EMMANUEL JOSEPH

The Mythic Clinic, Bridging Ancient Stories, Modern Medicine, and Architectural Design

Copyright © 2025 by Emmanuel Joseph

All rights reserved. No part of this publication may be reproduced, stored or transmitted in any form or by any means, electronic, mechanical, photocopying, recording, scanning, or otherwise without written permission from the publisher. It is illegal to copy this book, post it to a website, or distribute it by any other means without permission.

First edition

This book was professionally typeset on Reedsy.
Find out more at reedsy.com

# Contents

1 Chapter 1: The Roots of Healing ... 1
2 Chapter 2: The Renaissance of Medicine ... 3
3 Chapter 3: The Enlightenment and Rational Medicine ... 5
4 Chapter 4: The Industrial Revolution and Medical Progress ... 7
5 Chapter 5: The 20th Century: A New Era in Medicine ... 9
6 Chapter 6: The Role of Architecture in Healing ... 11
7 Chapter 7: Holistic Healing in Modern Times ... 12
8 Chapter 8: The Digital Age and Telemedicine ... 14
9 Chapter 9: The Healing Power of Design ... 16
10 Chapter 10: The Future of Medicine and Myth ... 18
11 Chapter 11: The Role of Community in Healing ... 20
12 Chapter 12: Bridging Ancient Stories, Modern Medicine, and... ... 22
13 Chapter 13: Integrative Medicine and Its Impact ... 24
14 Chapter 14: The Intersection of Art and Medicine ... 26
15 Chapter 15: The Future of Healthcare: A Vision for Tomorrow ... 28

# 1

# Chapter 1: The Roots of Healing

In the early days of human civilization, healing was an art closely intertwined with myth and religion. The first healers were often shamans, priests, or medicine men and women who called upon the gods, nature, and the cosmos to cure ailments. These early practitioners used rituals, chants, and herbal remedies passed down through generations. Ancient stories of miraculous recoveries were common, where divine intervention was credited for the healing. The belief in the supernatural played a crucial role in the perception and practice of medicine, making it not just a science but also a spiritual journey.

Over time, these early forms of healing evolved, influenced by the stories and myths of different cultures. From the ancient Greeks with their gods of healing like Asclepius, to the Chinese with their yin and yang balance in Traditional Chinese Medicine, these narratives provided a framework for understanding health and disease. The myths served as a bridge between the known and the unknown, giving people a sense of control over their health. The interplay between myth and medicine was not just about curing the body but also about healing the mind and spirit.

As civilizations grew, so did the knowledge and sophistication of their medical practices. The development of written language allowed for the recording and sharing of medical knowledge across generations and cultures. Ancient texts like the Hippocratic Corpus and the Ayurvedic scriptures became cornerstones of medical education. These texts combined empirical observation with mythic elements, reflecting the holistic approach to health that was prevalent in ancient societies. The integration of myth and medicine created a rich tapestry of healing practices that laid the foundation for modern medicine.

Despite the advancements in medical knowledge, the mythic elements of healing persisted. The belief in the power of the mind over the body, the placebo effect, and the influence of cultural narratives on health behaviors are all remnants of this ancient interplay. The roots of healing are deeply embedded in our collective consciousness, reminding us that the journey to wellness is as much about the stories we tell ourselves as it is about the treatments we receive.

# 2

# Chapter 2: The Renaissance of Medicine

The Renaissance period marked a significant turning point in the history of medicine. It was a time of rediscovery, innovation, and transformation, driven by a renewed interest in the classical knowledge of ancient Greece and Rome. Scholars and physicians began to question traditional beliefs and sought to understand the human body through observation and experimentation. This era saw the birth of modern anatomy, with pioneers like Andreas Vesalius who meticulously dissected human bodies and documented their findings in detailed anatomical drawings.

The Renaissance was also a time of great artistic and architectural achievements. The fusion of art and science during this period is exemplified by the work of Leonardo da Vinci, who not only created masterpieces of art but also conducted groundbreaking studies of human anatomy. His anatomical sketches, based on dissections he performed, revealed the intricate structures of the body and laid the groundwork for future medical advancements. The Renaissance clinic was a place where the lines between art, science, and mythology blurred, creating a holistic approach to healing.

In addition to the anatomical discoveries, the Renaissance brought about significant advancements in medical knowledge and practices. The development of the scientific method allowed physicians to systematically study diseases and develop effective treatments. The printing press played a crucial role in disseminating medical knowledge, making it accessible to a wider audience. Medical schools and universities flourished, attracting scholars from across Europe who contributed to the growing body of medical literature.

The architectural design of medical institutions during the Renaissance reflected the holistic approach to healing. Hospitals and clinics were often designed with large windows to allow natural light, open courtyards for fresh air, and beautiful gardens for patients to relax and rejuvenate. The incorporation of art and beauty into these spaces was believed to have a therapeutic effect on patients, promoting both physical and mental well-being. The Renaissance period was a time of great innovation and progress in medicine, laying the foundation for the modern medical practices we have today.

# 3

# Chapter 3: The Enlightenment and Rational Medicine

The Enlightenment era, also known as the Age of Reason, brought a new approach to medicine that emphasized rationality, empirical evidence, and scientific inquiry. Physicians and scientists sought to understand the underlying mechanisms of diseases and develop treatments based on observation and experimentation. This period saw the rise of clinical medicine, where careful examination and diagnosis became central to medical practice. The Enlightenment marked a shift away from the mythic and supernatural elements of healing towards a more systematic and evidence-based approach.

One of the most significant developments during the Enlightenment was the discovery of vaccination. Edward Jenner's work on smallpox vaccination in the late 18th century revolutionized the field of medicine and laid the groundwork for modern immunology. The success of vaccination demonstrated the power of scientific research and paved the way for the development of vaccines for other infectious diseases. This period also saw advancements in surgery, with the introduction of anesthesia and antiseptic techniques that greatly improved patient outcomes.

The architectural design of medical institutions during the Enlightenment reflected the principles of rationality and order. Hospitals were designed to be efficient and functional, with separate wards for different types of patients and specialized areas for surgery and treatment. The emphasis on cleanliness and hygiene became paramount, leading to the development of modern hospital sanitation practices. The Enlightenment clinic was a place of scientific inquiry, where the focus was on understanding and treating diseases through empirical evidence and rational thought.

Despite the emphasis on rationality, the influence of ancient myths and stories continued to permeate the practice of medicine. The human desire for meaning and connection to something greater than oneself persisted, even in the face of scientific advancements. The stories of miraculous recoveries and the power of the mind over the body continued to shape the way people perceived health and healing. The Enlightenment era was a time of great progress in medicine, but it also highlighted the enduring connection between myth, medicine, and the human experience.

# 4

# Chapter 4: The Industrial Revolution and Medical Progress

The Industrial Revolution brought about profound changes in society, technology, and medicine. The rapid advancements in industrial and scientific knowledge during the 19th century transformed the way diseases were understood and treated. The discovery of germ theory by Louis Pasteur and Robert Koch revolutionized the field of microbiology and led to the development of new methods for preventing and treating infectious diseases. The Industrial Revolution marked the beginning of modern medicine, where scientific research and technological innovation played a central role.

The development of new medical technologies and treatments during the Industrial Revolution greatly improved patient care. The invention of the stethoscope, X-rays, and other diagnostic tools allowed physicians to better understand the human body and diagnose diseases with greater accuracy. Surgical techniques also advanced, with the introduction of antiseptics and anesthesia reducing the risk of infection and pain during surgery. The Industrial Revolution clinic was a place of technological innovation, where the latest medical advancements were applied to improve patient outcomes.

The architectural design of medical institutions during the Industrial Revolution reflected the growing importance of technology and efficiency.

Hospitals and clinics were often large, multi-story buildings equipped with the latest medical equipment and facilities. The emphasis on cleanliness and hygiene continued to be a priority, with dedicated spaces for sterilization and sanitation. The Industrial Revolution also saw the development of specialized hospitals and clinics, such as maternity hospitals and mental asylums, reflecting the increasing specialization within the medical field.

Despite the rapid progress in medical technology and knowledge, the connection to ancient myths and stories remained. The human desire for meaning and connection to something greater than oneself continued to shape the way people perceived health and healing. The stories of miraculous recoveries and the power of the mind over the body persisted, even in the face of scientific advancements. The Industrial Revolution was a time of great progress in medicine, but it also highlighted the enduring connection between myth, medicine, and the human experience.

# 5

# Chapter 5: The 20th Century: A New Era in Medicine

The 20th century ushered in a new era of medical advancements and discoveries that transformed healthcare. The development of antibiotics, such as penicillin, revolutionized the treatment of infectious diseases and saved countless lives. The discovery of DNA and the understanding of genetics opened up new possibilities for diagnosing and treating inherited diseases. The 20th century saw the rise of modern medical research, with institutions dedicated to studying and combating diseases at a molecular level.

Advancements in medical technology during the 20th century further improved patient care. The invention of imaging technologies, such as MRI and CT scans, allowed physicians to see inside the human body with unprecedented clarity. Minimally invasive surgical techniques, such as laparoscopy, reduced recovery times and improved patient outcomes. The development of organ transplantation and the discovery of immunosuppressive drugs opened up new possibilities for treating end-stage organ failure. The 20th century clinic was a place of cutting-edge technology and innovation.

The architectural design of medical institutions during the 20th century reflected the emphasis on technology and patient-centered care. Hospitals were designed with modern amenities and facilities, including specialized units for different medical conditions. The focus on patient comfort and well-being became a priority, with the incorporation of natural light, green spaces, and art into hospital design. The 20th century also saw the rise of outpatient clinics and day surgery centers, providing patients with convenient and accessible healthcare options.

Despite the rapid progress in medical knowledge and technology, the connection to ancient myths and stories persisted. The human desire for meaning and connection to something greater than oneself continued to shape the way people perceived health and healing. The stories of miraculous recoveries and the power of the mind over the body remained, even in the face of scientific advancements. The 20th century was a time of great progress in medicine, but it also highlighted the enduring connection between myth, medicine, and the human experience.

# 6

# Chapter 6: The Role of Architecture in Healing

The design of healthcare facilities plays a crucial role in the healing process. Architecture can influence patient outcomes, staff efficiency, and overall well-being. The concept of therapeutic architecture emphasizes the importance of creating environments that promote healing and reduce stress. Natural light, green spaces, and art into hospital design. The 20th century also saw the rise of outpatient clinics and day surgery centers, providing patients with convenient and accessible healthcare options.

Despite the rapid progress in medical knowledge and technology, the connection to ancient myths and stories persisted. The human desire for meaning and connection to something greater than oneself continued to shape the way people perceived health and healing. The stories of miraculous recoveries and the power of the mind over the body remained, even in the face of scientific advancements. The 20th century was a time of great progress in medicine, but it also highlighted the enduring connection between myth, medicine, and the human experience.

# 7

# Chapter 7: Holistic Healing in Modern Times

The late 20th and early 21st centuries witnessed a resurgence of holistic healing practices that integrate ancient wisdom with modern medicine. This era saw a growing recognition of the importance of mental, emotional, and spiritual health in overall well-being. Practices such as yoga, meditation, acupuncture, and herbal medicine gained popularity as complementary therapies to conventional medical treatments. The holistic approach to healing emphasized the interconnectedness of the mind, body, and spirit, drawing on ancient stories and traditions for guidance.

The integration of holistic healing practices into modern medicine led to the development of integrative medicine, which combines the best of both worlds. Physicians and healthcare providers began to recognize the value of addressing the whole person, rather than just treating symptoms. This approach often involves collaboration between conventional medical practitioners and complementary therapy practitioners, creating a comprehensive and patient-centered care model. The modern clinic became a place where ancient healing traditions and cutting-edge medical treatments coexisted, offering patients a diverse range of options for their health and well-being.

Architectural design played a significant role in supporting holistic healing practices. Modern healthcare facilities began to incorporate elements that

## CHAPTER 7: HOLISTIC HEALING IN MODERN TIMES

promote relaxation, reduce stress, and enhance the healing environment. Features such as healing gardens, meditation rooms, and natural light became integral parts of hospital and clinic design. The emphasis on creating a calming and supportive environment for patients and staff reflected the holistic philosophy of treating the whole person. The integration of nature, art, and beauty into medical spaces contributed to the overall sense of well-being and healing.

The stories and myths that have shaped healing practices throughout history continued to inspire modern holistic healing. The belief in the power of the mind, the importance of balance and harmony, and the connection to nature are all themes that resonate in both ancient and modern healing traditions. As we move forward, the fusion of ancient wisdom and modern medicine offers a promising path for the future of healthcare, where the best of both worlds can be harnessed to promote health and well-being.

# 8

# Chapter 8: The Digital Age and Telemedicine

The advent of the digital age has revolutionized healthcare, bringing about significant advancements in telemedicine and digital health technologies. Telemedicine allows patients to receive medical consultations and treatments remotely, using video conferencing and digital communication tools. This technology has made healthcare more accessible, especially for individuals in remote or underserved areas. The digital clinic has become a vital component of modern healthcare, providing patients with convenient and efficient access to medical care.

Telemedicine has also facilitated the development of personalized medicine, where treatments and interventions are tailored to individual patients based on their unique genetic makeup, lifestyle, and medical history. The use of big data, artificial intelligence, and machine learning in healthcare has enabled physicians to analyze vast amounts of information and make more informed decisions about patient care. The digital age has brought about a paradigm shift in medicine, where data-driven approaches and technology play a central role in diagnosis, treatment, and prevention.

The architectural design of healthcare facilities in the digital age reflects the integration of technology and patient-centered care. Hospitals and clinics are equipped with advanced digital infrastructure, including telemedicine suites, electronic health record systems, and smart medical devices. The emphasis on creating flexible and adaptable spaces allows healthcare providers to seamlessly incorporate new technologies and innovations into their practice. The digital clinic is a dynamic and evolving space that leverages technology to enhance patient care and improve outcomes.

Despite the rapid advancements in digital health, the human element of healthcare remains essential. The stories and myths that have shaped healing practices throughout history continue to influence the way patients and providers perceive and experience health and wellness. The digital age offers new opportunities to bridge ancient wisdom with modern medicine, creating a holistic and integrated approach to healthcare. As we navigate the future of healthcare, the fusion of technology and human connection will be key to achieving the best possible outcomes for patients.

# 9

# Chapter 9: The Healing Power of Design

The design of healthcare facilities has a profound impact on the healing process, influencing patient outcomes, staff efficiency, and overall well-being. The concept of therapeutic architecture emphasizes the importance of creating environments that promote healing, reduce stress, and enhance the patient experience. Elements such as natural light, green spaces, art, and calming colors are incorporated into healthcare design to create a supportive and healing environment.

The integration of nature into healthcare facilities, known as biophilic design, has been shown to have numerous benefits for patients and staff. Access to natural light, views of nature, and indoor plants can reduce stress, improve mood, and enhance overall well-being. Healing gardens and outdoor spaces provide patients with a place to relax and connect with nature, promoting physical and mental recovery. The use of natural materials, such as wood and stone, also creates a warm and welcoming atmosphere that contributes to the healing process.

Art and aesthetics play a significant role in healthcare design, with research showing that art can have a positive impact on patient outcomes. Art can provide a sense of comfort, distraction, and inspiration, helping to reduce anxiety and improve the overall patient experience. The incorporation of local culture and community into healthcare design can also create a sense of belonging and connection, making patients feel more at ease. The healing power of design extends beyond the physical environment, influencing the emotional and psychological well-being of patients and staff.

The stories and myths that have shaped healing practices throughout history continue to inspire modern healthcare design. The belief in the healing power of nature, the importance of beauty and harmony, and the connection to something greater than oneself are all themes that resonate in both ancient and modern healing traditions. As we move forward, the integration of therapeutic architecture and design into healthcare will play a crucial role in promoting health and well-being for patients and staff alike.

# 10

# Chapter 10: The Future of Medicine and Myth

As we look to the future of medicine, the fusion of ancient wisdom and modern technology offers a promising path forward. The integration of holistic healing practices, personalized medicine, and digital health technologies has the potential to revolutionize healthcare and improve patient outcomes. The future clinic will be a place where the best of both worlds come together, creating a comprehensive and patient-centered approach to health and well-being.

The use of big data, artificial intelligence, and genomics will continue to drive advancements in personalized medicine, allowing for more precise and effective treatments. Telemedicine and digital health technologies will make healthcare more accessible and convenient, especially for individuals in remote or underserved areas. The integration of complementary therapies, such as acupuncture, meditation, and herbal medicine, will provide patients with a diverse range of options for their health and well-being. The future clinic will be a dynamic and evolving space that leverages technology and ancient wisdom to promote health and healing.

The architectural design of healthcare facilities in the future will continue to prioritize the patient experience and support the healing process. The use of biophilic design, art, and aesthetics will create environments that promote

## CHAPTER 10: THE FUTURE OF MEDICINE AND MYTH

well-being and reduce stress. The integration of technology, such as smart medical devices and digital health platforms, will enhance patient care and improve outcomes. The future clinic will be a place where the principles of therapeutic architecture and design are applied to create a holistic and supportive environment for patients and staff.

The stories and myths that have shaped healing practices throughout history will continue to influence the future of medicine. The belief in the power of the mind, the importance of balance and harmony, and the connection to something greater than oneself are all themes that resonate in both ancient and modern healing traditions. As we navigate the future of healthcare, the fusion of myth, medicine, and architectural design will create a comprehensive and integrated approach to health and well-being.

# 11

# Chapter 11: The Role of Community in Healing

The importance of community in the healing process cannot be overstated. Social support, connection, and a sense of belonging are essential for overall well-being and recovery. The concept of community healing emphasizes the role of relationships and social networks in promoting health and resilience. From ancient times to the present, the power of community has been a central theme in healing practices, reflecting the interconnectedness of individuals and their social environment.

In modern healthcare, the role of community is increasingly recognized as a vital component of patient care. Support groups, peer networks, and community resources provide patients with emotional and practical support, helping them navigate their health journeys. The integration of community health workers and patient advocates into healthcare teams ensures that patients have access to the resources and support they need. The modern clinic is not just a place for medical treatment but also a hub for community engagement and support.

The architectural design of healthcare facilities can play a significant role in fostering a sense of community and connection. The incorporation of communal spaces, such as waiting areas, lounges, and gardens, provides patients and families with opportunities to connect and support one another.

## CHAPTER 11: THE ROLE OF COMMUNITY IN HEALING

The use of local art and cultural elements in healthcare design can create a sense of identity and belonging, making patients feel more at ease. The creation of welcoming and inclusive spaces reflects the importance of community in the healing process.

The stories and myths that have shaped healing practices throughout history continue to inspire the role of community in modern healthcare. The belief in the power of collective support, the importance of social connection, and the role of community in promoting health and well-being are all themes that resonate in both ancient and modern healing traditions. As we move forward, the integration of community healing into healthcare will be essential for promoting overall health and resilience.

# 12

# Chapter 12: Bridging Ancient Stories, Modern Medicine, and Architectural Design

Modern technology, offers a promising path forward. The integration of holistic healing practices, personalized medicine, and digital health technologies has the potential to revolutionize healthcare and improve patient outcomes. The future clinic will be a place where the best of both worlds come together, creating a comprehensive and patient-centered approach to health and well-being.

The use of big data, artificial intelligence, and genomics will continue to drive advancements in personalized medicine, allowing for more precise and effective treatments. Telemedicine and digital health technologies will make healthcare more accessible and convenient, especially for individuals in remote or underserved areas. The integration of complementary therapies, such as acupuncture, meditation, and herbal medicine, will provide patients with a diverse range of options for their health and well-being. The future clinic will be a dynamic and evolving space that leverages technology and ancient wisdom to promote health and healing.

The architectural design of healthcare facilities in the future will continue to prioritize the patient experience and support the healing process. The use of biophilic design, art, and aesthetics will create environments that promote well-being and reduce stress. The integration of technology, such as smart medical devices and digital health platforms, will enhance patient care and improve outcomes. The future clinic will be a place where the principles of therapeutic architecture and design are applied to create a holistic and supportive environment for patients and staff.

The stories and myths that have shaped healing practices throughout history will continue to influence the future of medicine. The belief in the power of the mind, the importance of balance and harmony, and the connection to something greater than oneself are all themes that resonate in both ancient and modern healing traditions. As we navigate the future of healthcare, the fusion of myth, medicine, and architectural design will create a comprehensive and integrated approach to health and well-being.

# 13

# Chapter 13: Integrative Medicine and Its Impact

Integrative medicine is a holistic approach that combines conventional medical treatments with complementary therapies to address the whole person. This approach recognizes the interconnectedness of the mind, body, and spirit and seeks to promote overall well-being. Integrative medicine incorporates practices such as acupuncture, herbal medicine, yoga, and mindfulness meditation alongside conventional treatments to create a comprehensive and patient-centered care plan.

The rise of integrative medicine has been driven by a growing recognition of the limitations of conventional medicine in addressing chronic diseases and complex health conditions. Patients and healthcare providers alike have sought out alternative and complementary therapies to fill the gaps in conventional care. Integrative medicine emphasizes the importance of lifestyle factors, such as diet, exercise, and stress management, in maintaining health and preventing disease. This approach has been shown to improve patient outcomes and satisfaction, offering a more holistic and personalized approach to healthcare.

Architectural design plays a crucial role in supporting integrative medicine. Healthcare facilities that incorporate elements of nature, art, and beauty create a healing environment that complements the holistic approach to care.

Spaces designed for relaxation, meditation, and movement provide patients with opportunities to engage in complementary therapies and promote overall well-being. The design of integrative medicine clinics reflects the principles of balance, harmony, and connection that are central to this approach.

The stories and myths that have shaped healing practices throughout history continue to inspire integrative medicine. The belief in the power of the mind, the importance of balance and harmony, and the connection to nature are all themes that resonate in both ancient and modern healing traditions. Integrative medicine offers a promising path forward for healthcare, where the best of both worlds come together to promote health and well-being.

# 14

# Chapter 14: The Intersection of Art and Medicine

Art and medicine have been intertwined throughout history, with art playing a significant role in medical education, diagnosis, and treatment. From ancient anatomical drawings to modern medical illustrations, art has provided a visual representation of the human body and its functions. The intersection of art and medicine has also extended to the therapeutic use of art in healing, with practices such as art therapy gaining recognition as effective complementary treatments.

Medical illustrations and anatomical drawings have been essential tools in medical education, helping students and practitioners understand the complex structures of the human body. The work of artists like Leonardo da Vinci and Andreas Vesalius has provided invaluable insights into human anatomy and laid the groundwork for modern medical knowledge. The use of art in medical education continues to evolve, with digital technology enabling the creation of detailed and interactive visual representations of the body.

Art therapy is a complementary treatment that uses creative expression to promote emotional and psychological healing. This practice has been shown to reduce stress, improve mood, and enhance overall well-being. Art therapy provides patients with a non-verbal outlet for expressing their emotions and experiences, offering a unique and valuable addition to conventional medical treatments. The use of art in healing reflects the holistic approach to healthcare that recognizes the importance of the mind and spirit in overall well-being.

The architectural design of healthcare facilities can support the integration of art and medicine by incorporating art into the physical environment. Hospitals and clinics that display artwork, create healing gardens, and provide spaces for creative expression create a supportive and healing atmosphere for patients and staff. The use of art in healthcare design reflects the principles of beauty, harmony, and connection that are central to the holistic approach to healing. The intersection of art and medicine continues to inspire and enhance the practice of healthcare, offering a unique and valuable perspective on healing.

# 15

# Chapter 15: The Future of Healthcare: A Vision for Tomorrow

As we look to the future of healthcare, the integration of ancient wisdom, modern medicine, and innovative design offers a promising path forward. The future clinic will be a place where the best of both worlds come together, creating a comprehensive and patient-centered approach to health and well-being. Advances in technology, personalized medicine, and holistic healing practices will drive the evolution of healthcare, offering new possibilities for diagnosis, treatment, and prevention.

The use of big data, artificial intelligence, and genomics will continue to revolutionize personalized medicine, allowing for more precise and effective treatments. Telemedicine and digital health technologies will make healthcare more accessible and convenient, especially for individuals in remote or underserved areas. The integration of complementary therapies, such as acupuncture, meditation, and herbal medicine, will provide patients with a diverse range of options for their health and well-being. The future clinic will be a dynamic and evolving space that leverages technology and ancient wisdom to promote health and healing.

The architectural design of healthcare facilities in the future will prioritize the patient experience and support the healing process. The use of biophilic design, art, and aesthetics will create environments that promote well-being and reduce stress. The integration of technology, such as smart medical devices and digital health platforms, will enhance patient care and improve outcomes. The future clinic will be a place where the principles of therapeutic architecture and design are applied to create a holistic and supportive environment for patients and staff.

The stories and myths that have shaped healing practices throughout history will continue to influence the future of medicine. The belief in the power of the mind, the importance of balance and harmony, and the connection to something greater than oneself are all themes that resonate in both ancient and modern healing traditions. As we navigate the future of healthcare, the fusion of myth, medicine, and architectural design will create a comprehensive and integrated approach to health and well-being.

**Book Description:**

**The Mythic Clinic: Bridging Ancient Stories, Modern Medicine, and Architectural Design** is an exploration of the fascinating interplay between myth, medicine, and architecture throughout history. This book delves into the ancient roots of healing, the Renaissance's artistic and scientific breakthroughs, the rational approach of the Enlightenment, the technological advancements of the Industrial Revolution, and the holistic practices of modern times. It examines how architectural design has influenced the healing process and how the integration of art and nature into healthcare spaces can enhance well-being. As we look to the future of medicine, this book envisions a world where ancient wisdom and modern technology come together to create a comprehensive and patient-centered approach to healthcare. Through twelve chapters, each filled with detailed insights and historical context, **The Mythic Clinic** offers a unique and inspiring perspective on the evolution of medicine and the enduring power of myth in healing.

www.ingramcontent.com/pod-product-compliance
Lightning Source LLC
LaVergne TN
LVHW020741090526
838202LV00057BA/6160